adapted by Brian Gleeson

PECOS BILL

illustrated by Tim Raglin

Rabbit Ears Books

There aren't that many cowboys these days, not real ones like Pecos Bill. Bill was a piece of work, all right. He was the dog-gonedest, gol-dingedest, dad-blamedest son of the prairie sod who ever rode across these here United States. Any cow puncher worth a lick will tell you that if it weren't for Bill, there wouldn't have been a Wild West. It would have been plain old mundane.

It took a man like Pecos Bill to conquer the West. Before he came on the scene cowboys didn't know a thing about cows. And let me tell you, a cowboy who doesn't know about cows is pretty lame. But we're putting our socks on over our boots here, sliding down the hill before we know where the cactus are, getting a little bit ahead of ourselves. Because to understand what Bill was about, you've got to know he was half coyote.

Bill started out his life just like you and me. He was the youngest of fourteen brothers and sisters and his folks lived right smack in the middle of Texas. They were your regular family of prairie settlers, except Bill's father had a powerful fear of getting hemmed in by neighbors.

When Bill was only a couple of weeks old, his father decided the family was going to move. Some other family had moved in right next door, only two hundred miles away.

"If it's one thing I can't stand," said Bill's father, "it's being cramped by squatters."

So Bill's family piled into their Conestoga wagon and headed west. They had traveled in that wagon for two weeks when, quite by accident, little Bill squirted out the back. Since pioneers were busy pioneering all the time, Bill's parents didn't realize he was gone until they took a head count three weeks later. By that time, they decided to chalk up the loss of their youngest son to experience, and didn't bother backtracking to find the little devil.

So there was poor Bill, a mere babe, all alone on the range. His parents and his brothers and his sisters were gone forever. Pecos Bill's prospects looked mighty slim.

Luckily, the first critter to happen upon Bill was a coyote. Like all coyotes, this one had a soft spot for young'uns, so she took him to her den. There, Bill grew up just like a coyote – a darn good coyote, too.

Young Bill learned to run across the plains, kicking up clouds of dust faster than a jackrabbit. He was so fast he could outrun a deer when the two of them played tag. Mostly he played fair with the other coyotes, although from time to time he did take advantage of them.

He was especially good at the sing-alongs at night when all the coyotes would go up on the ridge and howl at the moon. There was no end to the fun Bill had growing up with the coyotes. That was the life! Bill was a coyote through and through, born to be wild.

One day, Bill was scouting down by the Pecos River looking for his coyote buddies when he came across the strangest creature. Mind you, Bill had never seen a cowboy before because he was a coyote and coyotes have no time for humans. So Bill sidled up to the cowboy coyote-style and investigated the situation. Bill had never seen anything like this sorry dude before.

The cowboy couldn't believe his eyes either. Because, as you can imagine, Bill was quite a sight for the stranger to behold. He looked down at Bill from his horse and said, "You're as naked as a jaybird, partner! Why in tarnation are you running around without your clothes? Did you lose them in a poker game or something?"

"What do you mean naked?" Bill howled. "I'm a coyote, and coyotes don't wear no clothes."

"That'll be the day," said the cowboy. "You're no coyote. Shucks, you don't even have a tail. You are a human being."

Bill turned his head to look down along his backside and, by jeepers, he didn't have a tail! But he still was not completely convinced. After all, he was happy to be a coyote.

"But I've got fleas and howl at the moon at night," Bill replied.

"Aw, g'wan," said the cowboy with a laugh. "Everybody knows that all Texicans got fleas and howl at the moon."

Bill didn't want to believe he was no longer a coyote, but this stranger had made several good points. The cowboy was a neighborly sort, so he gave Bill the extra set of duds he kept in his saddlebag. And as soon as Bill put on these clothes, it was like he was a natural-born cowboy. It took Bill an hour to learn how to talk. Back in those days, coyote lingo and Texican lingo were almost the same language. He had only fifty words to learn.

Bill had woke up thinking he was a coyote, and by sundown he was a walking, talking cowboy. Naturally he still had more than a few coyote notions left in him. It ended up being a pretty full day for Pecos Bill.

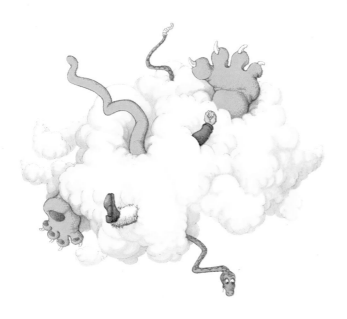

Bill didn't waste any time and set right out across the range to find out what it was like being a cowboy. Before he got too far, he was surprised by a forty-two foot rattlesnake sunning himself on a rock. That rattler saw Bill and figured it was lunch time. But old Bill had another idea.

"I needed a rope, and now I've got one!" Bill cried with delight. "It's got a rattle attached to it, too!"

Once he found his rope, Bill decided he needed a critter to ride. Up in the hills, he bumped into a cougar that was two tons bigger than any horse and he knew he was in business.

Bill jumped on the cat's back, heeled him in the ribs and gave him a loud, "Giddap!" That cougar didn't take too kindly to his coyote-cowboy passenger; but then again, the cat didn't have too much to say about it.

Day and night, Bill rode his snarling cougar and twirled his rattlesnake rope and generally whooped it up. On the twelfth day, he came across a cowboy camp. Now, Bill had worked up quite an appetite on his little ride, so he made a beeline for the campfire. He swallowed a whole kettle of porkbelly and beans. Then he washed it down with a pot of boiling hot coffee. And when he was done with chow, he wiped his mouth with a hunk of cactus. Coyotes, unlike cowboys, are always tidy when they dine.

Never one for fancy introductions, Bill stood there looking at the cowboys and inquired, "Who's the boss around here?"

These cowboys, as tough and as hard as they were, had never seen a buckeroo like Bill. They knew right off that they were in the company of someone a little different. The ugliest and meanest of these cowpokes was named Sourdough. He was so nasty that all the other cowboys let him be the boss because they didn't want to look him in the eye to tell him otherwise. Now Sourdough ambled up to Pecos and the two of them stood there face-to-face.

"I was the boss… till you showed up," said Sourdough, sweet as honey. "Partner, that was the ding-dandiest display I've ever seen. I reckon you're the boss man now."

"What do you fellers do, anyway?" Bill asked.

"Not much," said Sourdough. "We eat beans, and we ride around a bit. Other than that, it's pretty slow 'round these parts."

"Then what do you do with all these cows?" said Bill.

"We got so many of 'em, we don't know what to do with 'em all," Sourdough replied.

"Well, if you boys aren't dumb as dirt," said Bill, who was always thinking. "Let's take these cows up to Kansas! Folks up there could use them as pets. Least-ways, it'll give us something to do."

And just like that, easy as pie, Bill had invented the cattle drive. Bill and his men commenced marching those cows right up to Kansas, or bust!

Riding his cougar mount on the cattle drive just wasn't working out for Bill after awhile. The longhorns, not to mention the other cowpokes, were getting mighty spooked and acting like regular Nervous Nells around the cat. Bill needed a new mount. And as soon as Bill spotted this one wild mustang, he knew he had found his perfect riding companion. That mustang had a history of being the most ornery critter in the West. The cowboys called him Widow-Maker, since riding him was the last thing a feller did.

"That's just the kind of sweet little hossie I want," Bill said as he rubbed his hands together. Off Bill ran after that mustang, like a coyote chasing the wind.

"No polecat is going to ride my back," Widow-Maker said in horse lingo, which, of course, Bill knew frontwards and backwards.

As fast as Widow-Maker galloped, Bill still managed to overtake him. You can imagine how this surprised the unsociable mustang.

"Why don't we just team up, and get it over with so we can whoop it up together?" Bill said to Widow-Maker.

Widow-Maker gave Bill a sniff and figured that if anyone had to ride him, it might as well be a cowboy who was half coyote. After that the two of them were quick partners. Widow-Maker had dynamite in his hooves and nitroglycerine in his veins. Only one man could ride him, let alone understand him, and that was Pecos Bill.

In those days, cowboys weren't too good at rounding up cattle. It was up to Pecos Bill to show his cowboys how a real buckeroo worked a cattle drive.

One day a cowboy in his crew followed a stray steer to the top of a mountain and got stranded. Down on the flatlands, Bill got all the rope he could muster and lassoed his partner – and the steer – from the mountaintop.

The other cowpunchers on the cattle drive took to the new device and it became an important cowboy tool, especially for roping a steer by the horns. And that's how cowboys started using lariats.

The cattle sometimes got a might perturbed with Pecos, now that the shoe was on the other hoof. One day the biggest, most cantankerous steer decided to fix him for good. This steer, Old Blue was his name, lowered his horns, got Bill in his sights, and charged at him.

When Bill got a load of what was happening, he froze Old Blue right in mid-stride with his eyes. That steer was big, but he wasn't dumb. And now that Old Blue had time to think, he recognized that Bill wasn't all that bad.

After Bill unfroze him, Old Blue was the best steer they had on the cattle drive. Day after day, he always led the way for the rest of the cattle, pushing forward on the trail to Kansas.

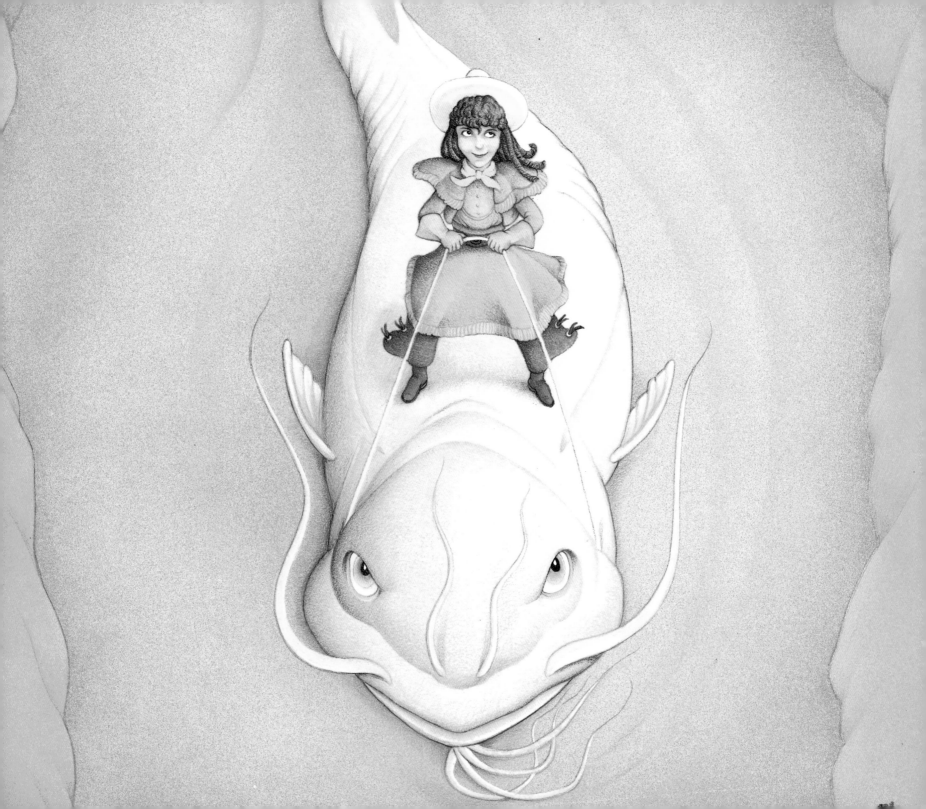

When the cattle drive got to the Rio Grande, Bill's life changed forever. Down the river came this independent little gal stand-up riding on the back of a fifty-three foot catfish! Even for Texas that was a pretty fair-sized catfish. That was the first time Bill laid eyes on Slue-Foot Sue.

"Whooa-wee, that's the purdiest girl in the world!" yipped Bill, who was reduced to a lovesick pup as soon as he saw Slue-Foot Sue. "I love you with all my heart," he told her. "I want to make you my wife."

Slue-Foot Sue was flattered by the proposal. The idea of spending the rest of her days with a prospect like Pecos Bill was mighty appealing.

"I'd be honored to be your lawful wife," Sue told Bill. "Why don't you finish this here cattle drive and I'll meet you in Kansas when you're done."

"And then we can get married, and live happily ever after," said Bill.

The two lovebirds parted ways, Sue riding her catfish down the Rio Grande, and Bill heading north with the cattle drive. Bill pushed on with a vengeance: The trail was dusty, the sun was scorching, the days were long…and that was the good part.

Every night when the sun went down behind the mountains, all the cowboys would gather around the campfire to whittle and play a game of cards. Bill would tuck the cattle into bed, and then he'd wander off to a high ridge to howl at the moon.

Maybe Bill went off to howl because he was longing for Sue; maybe he needed to be by himself for a spell; or maybe he missed his coyote family. But there was one thing for certain: Howling at the moon was something Bill just had to do.

For five months the cattle drive pushed on until finally Bill and his cowboys were less than a day's ride from the Kansas border. It was time to celebrate: The end of the drive was near.

Bill gave the fellers the rest of the day off and they held a hootenanny with singing and dancing. They were having a foot-stompin' good time when, right in the middle of a do-si-do, the biggest cyclone ever seen in the West darkened the horizon.

The twister, swirling around at five hundred miles an hour and sucking up everything in its path, was heading right toward the cattle. Bill knew in his bones he had to do something. He threw his lariat and lassoed the cyclone by the neck. Widow-Maker and Bill tried with all their might to pull it down, but this was no ordinary tornado.

The cyclone snapped its head forward and Bill shot off Widow-Maker. He hung on to the rope and dug his heels into the plains to get the twister under control. But there was nothing doing. The cyclone stopped short and the backlash yanked Bill smack onto his back.

"All right, you big bag of wind," hollered Bill. "Show me what you can do! Yeeeeee-ha!"

Bill had the ride of his life on that twister. The two of them bucked and rolled and clawed so hard they dug out the Grand Canyon.

Bill tried to knock out the cyclone by riding it into a mountain, but the twister just ripped off the mountaintop and rode on through.

The cyclone spun faster and faster to try to get Bill to loosen his grip. Fat chance! All that cyclone ended up doing was fanning the lakes dry. Now that made Bill mad. Bill pulled so tight with his rope that he made the cyclone cry. That twister bawled so hard its tears welled up and made the Great Salt Lake.

Out onto the Gulf of Mexico the twister went, tail-dancing across the water like a King salmon. Bill gave a crank and the twister rolled on its back, crazier than a bronc on locoweed, scraping the land flat. Folks called that spot Death Valley from then on, because nothing ever lived there after Bill and the twister were done with it.

But Bill hung on. And they went back and forth like that for ten full days until Bill finally managed to steer the twister up toward the heavens. Up and up they went riding through the clouds, up and up...and...

That was the last anybody ever heard of Bill.

Well, the cowboys got the cattle drive to Kansas and from then on cowboys always made cattle drives, just the way Bill taught them.

Now don't you go feeling sorry for Bill. He would have laughed at you for being so sentimental. After all, Bill isn't really gone. If you go out to west Texas, you can still see Bill, if you try hard enough. Listen to the Wind, and when it starts to howl like a coyote, look high up in the sky.

I guarantee you that Pecos Bill and Slue-Foot Sue will be there, riding Widow-Maker across the heavens, jumping from cloud to cloud.